Allah, Your Mercy!

Before you start

My dear friends and fellow seekers of truth,

Welcome to a journey that I hope will transform your understanding of yourself and your spiritual life. This book is meant to be a companion to you as you explore the depths of your soul, seeking a deeper connection with the Divine. My heartfelt desire is to help you grow spiritually, to empower you on your quest for enlightenment.

For too long, we have been shaped by voices that often miss the true complexity of human existence. We are not just souls; we are beings with bodies, emotions, inclinations, and instincts. We are social creatures with desires, ambitions, and diverse needs that stretch beyond the purely spiritual.

Ignoring our multifaceted nature has led to many misunderstandings and caused many of us to lose our way. To reach genuine spiritual enlightenment and growth, we must understand how these dimensions interweave. Neglecting even one aspect can throw us off balance.

It's crucial to recognise that spiritual challenges aren't always solved by purely 'religious' solutions alone. Often, their roots lie in a complex mix of factors. Our existence is more complex than we can fully grasp. We are here to continue the cycle of life, passing on our essence to future generations and reuniting with our loved ones in the eternal gardens of Eden.

This series, titled 'Rectifications of Misconceptions,' aims to harmonise traditional religious wisdom with modern insights, striking a balance that nurtures both the soul and the mind.

Upcoming works in this series include:
- Deepfake Religiosity
- The Art of Perseverance
- The Benefits of Sincerity

However, the book you are currently holding is 'Sin, Guilt, and Repentance.'

Allow me to share some essential concepts that are central to our spiritual journey:

Spiritual darkness is a real state of the soul's despondency, stemming from separation from the Divine.

Self-discovery and spiritual growth are treasures awaiting those who embark on the journey within.

The paths to spiritual growth are as diverse as the individuals who walk them.

The time spent in spiritual darkness will affect the time needed for spiritual healing.

Not experiencing Allah's presence is at the core of spiritual darkness.

Salvation depends on our unwavering commitment to live a life reflecting divine virtues, thus escaping the traps of sin.

Entering Paradise hinges on divine mercy, forgiveness of sins, and an invitation to the heavenly abode.

In the divine court, was—flawed and unworthy—are declared righteous through faith alone.

Allah's love precedes our love for Him; we approach Him with hearts
ready to receive His grace and forgiveness.

Faith is a divine gift, and righteousness flows naturally from it.

Salvation should not be seen merely as a matter of performing rituals.

Finding Allah often starts with recognising our limitations and knowing that the answers lie beyond our individual abilities.

Acknowledging the complex web of factors causing spiritual desolation is the first step toward resolution.

Our physical condition affects our mental clarity and our soul's ability to
perceive beautiful, hopeful truths.

Spiritual depression is as real as the eternal truths underlying our faith.

We must resist turning justification by faith into justification by performance.

Our quest to find Allah begins with the realisation of our inadequacies and the understanding that the answers lie beyond ourselves.

May these insights and reflections light your path toward greater spiritual understanding and well-being.

The beginning of a journey

Allow me to share with you the remarkable journey that led me to write this book. When I embraced Islam three decades ago, I embarked on the memorisation of the Quran in the vast and serene deserts of Sudan. In the tranquil heart of the desert, I found the perfect environment to focus entirely on this sacred task. Those days were incredibly beautiful and transformative. I can still vividly recall being an eighteen-year-old, gazing up at the night sky, feeling overwhelmed with emotion.

The starlit canopy appeared as a divine gift from Allah—a breathtaking world that filled me with awe and wonder.

From there, my journey took me around the world in pursuit of knowledge, with the hope of discovering that one sentence that would change my heart, my soul, and my connection with the Almighty. I travelled from the mystical heart of Sudan, learning from its wise scholars, to the profound Moroccan scholars in Belgium to the knowledgeable syrian scholars in the Netherlands then I continued my travels to numerous masters in Saudi Arabia. One significant milestone in my journey led me to become the first convert ever to be employed by the Ministry of Islamic Affairs of the Hashemite Kingdom of Jordan. My role was to make the call to prayer, lead prayers, and deliver Friday sermons. I was also granted permission to pass on the ten Qira'at. This phase of my journey further enriched my understanding of Islam and spirituality.

Over more than two decades, I had the privilege to sit at the feet of these great teachers. This period gifted me numerous *ijāzāt* (teaching permissions) and *asānīd* (chains of narrations). As you can see, my beginnings were very traditional.

However, my path took an unexpected turn when I was invited to apply for a Master's degree in Islamic Mental Health. At the time, I was teaching at Rotterdam University for Applied Islamic Sciences and thought to myself, "Why not?" This turned out to be one of the best decisions I have ever made. Suddenly, the Quranic verses and thousands of *aḥadīth* I had memorised began to resonate more deeply with me.

This academic pursuit allowed me to approach these sacred texts from a unique perspective and to extract deeper meanings. It was as if I finally understood the saying of Ibn al-ʿArabī "Allah's knowledge is not restricted by yours." The more I delved into various sciences, the more profound my understanding of the Holy Quran became. Imam al-Rāzī is an excellent example of someone who harnessed different sciences to better understand the Quran, putting all sciences at service of interpreting the Holy Book.

As time went by and my lectures continued, my interest in mental health and spiritual development grew stronger. I began writing numerous articles, many of which have yet to be published. My explorations led me much further than I could have ever imagined. I spared no effort in my quest to delve into the essence of human existence, leaving no stone unturned, reading hundreds of books.

Within the framework of Islamic teachings, I engaged in multidisciplinary research, preparing myself to compile a comprehensive Spiritual Growth Programme. I expanded my knowledge and expertise, becoming a Psychotherapist with a degree in Neuroscience, Neuroplasticity, Advanced Cognitive

Behavioural Therapy (CBT), a Master of Neuro-Linguistic Programming, and a PhD in Islamic Sciences.

Even as I speak, I am still on a never-ending quest for more knowledge to contribute to the development of my Spiritual Growth Programme. What you have in your hands today is just a small piece of a larger puzzle, one of the many books that will soon be published as part of the series: "Rectifications of Islam Misconceptions." This series serves as a vital contribution to rectifying misconceptions about spirituality, religiosity, and the role of mental health in building a strong Islamic personality.

In our ever-evolving world, Five Golden Principles:

- Spiritual Growth
- Religious Empowerment
- Personal Development
- Mental Health
- Physical Well-being

are deeply interconnected. Each of these realities has its own principles, obstacles, catalysts, problems, and solutions. And it all begins with a correct and holistic understanding of these interconnected realities.

Imam Ibn al-Qayyim highlighted in *I'lām al-Muwaqqi'īn* that the personality of a jurist shines through his legal opinions and religious verdicts, while Imam Sha'rānī echoed this in his masterpiece al-Mīzān al-Kubrā.

Sadly enough, some preachers (and I am deliberately not saying scholars, teachers or masters) bring their personalities to the forefront without proper spiritual and religious training, leading to unbalanced and distorted perspectives, which inevitably influences their interpretation of Islam, understanding human reality, identifying problems and recommending solutions. I delve deeper into this matter in my book *Deepfake Religiosity*.

To address these issues, we must redefine Islamic terms and approach the human being from a holistic perspective, acknowledging that humans are more than just souls. That is exactly what we will be doing in this book: redefining sin and repentance from an Islamic and holistic perspective, inspired by tradition.

Repentance and Happiness

Amid our complex lives, the concept of happiness stands as a nebulous entity, ever evolving and eluding the grasp of many. Everyone, with their unique experiences and perspectives, seems to hold a distinct interpretation of what constitutes true happiness. However, it is evident that the vast majority remain in search of that elusive state of being.

Happiness—it is said—is as diverse as the countless souls inhabiting this planet. For some, it is derived from simple pleasures like dining at a fine restaurant, losing oneself in the pages of a compelling book, or sipping a mocktail by the river. These moments may evoke feelings of happiness, but they are transient, incapable of leaving a lasting contentment. Genuine happiness, on the other hand, resides deep within, untouched by external stimuli. It is a concept that may appear perplexing at first glance. How can *nothing* be the source of one's happiness? Allow me to explain myself.

The essence of happiness is not fleeting; it is a continuous, unshakable foundation that begins with a sense of inner satisfaction. It finds resonance in the Quranic verse

> Say: let it be with Allah's favour and His mercy that they rejoice themselves; this is better than what they keep on accumulating.[1]

The teachings of the noble Prophet Muhammad (peace be upon

---

[1] *Imam al Biqa'i said about this verse: "Spiritual happiness is better (more intense and satisfying) than physical happiness." (Nadhm ad durar fi tanasub al ayat was suwar, Q.10:58)*

him) further illuminate this path:

> Be satisfied with what you have, and you will be the most grateful of all.to [2]

This kind of happiness remains undisturbed by external adversities. It does not imply that external calamities will not inflict sadness; rather, it signifies that they shall not breach one's internal state of happiness. It is essential to acknowledge that certain circumstances, such as the loss of a child, a partner, or heinous acts like torture and abuse, can inflict wounds that are difficult to heal.

So, what constitutes being genuinely happy? It is intrinsically linked to the broader purpose of one's life. True happiness emerges when the spirit is in harmony with itself, the world, destiny, and Allah. It necessitates an amicable relationship with the Almighty. Regrettably, this is an area where many falter.

We invest in our physical well-being and material wealth but often neglect the well-being of our souls. A lack of alignment with the Divine, whether due to sin or a failure to repent, corrodes the soul from within. It gnaws at the core of our being, tearing us apart. We may attempt to disregard this disquiet, but it proves impossible to silence. It is the soul's restlessness, the anguish of being separated from its Source, its Creator, and its purpose. The Prophet Muhammad (peace be upon him) said:

> True happiness is the richness of the soul![3]

Psychologists propose that genuine happiness is derived from

---

[2] *Sunan ibn Maja: 4217, Makarim al_akhlaq, 224 al-Khara-iti, Musnad Shamiyin: 4208*
[3] *Musnad Ahmad: 431c, Sahih al-Bukhari: 244c, Sahih Muslim: 1051, Ibn Maja: 4137.*

leading a meaningful life, not merely a pleasurable one. When we bear witness to the *shahada* we make a conscious choice. We choose to exist in devotion to the afterlife, to serve Allah, following the path of His Prophet, and ultimately striving for a place in Paradise, an eternal abode.

We choose obedience over disobedience, knowing that the former leads to His pleasure while the latter incurs His displeasure. We choose to be part of a collective that serves the greater good, extending our hands to aid, advise, and contribute to the betterment of the world. When we fall short of these choices, a discontentment often runs deep within us, even if we remain unaware of it.

It is akin to those who, in a bid to shield themselves from the profound sorrow of losing a loved one or navigating a painful divorce, choose to numb their emotions. They may temporarily suppress their pain, but it inevitably resurfaces in the form of anger, hysteria, stress, depression, and an unexplainable sense of sadness and emptiness. When they eventually confront their loss and pain, they start the healing process, often shedding tears as if the wounds were freshly inflicted, even if years have passed.

Similarly, many Muslims unknowingly grapple with an inner unhappiness, outward stress, inner turmoil, and an inexplicable loneliness, as if something vital is amiss. This stems from the incongruity between the lives they lead and the choices they've made at a more subconscious level.

It is paramount to understand that failing to live in accordance with one's beliefs, particularly from a religious standpoint, can lead to depression, anxiety, sadness, uncertainty, and low self-esteem. Subconsciously, self-reproach prevails, and the feeling of insignificance takes over, regardless of one's achievements in the eyes of the world. The true measure of who we are becomes evident when we are alone, when we confront the dissonance between our chosen path and our actions.

Thus, intrinsic happiness is achieved by dissolving the dissonance that exists between our true selves and our actions. This journey towards harmony is embarked upon through repentance. Repentance is the vital bridge that connects us with a meaningful, purposeful life, wherein happiness is independent of material possessions. Rather, it hinges on our fidelity to the path we have chosen.

Repentance allows you to find a meaningful, purposeful life where your happiness doesn't depend on what you have but on how much you live up to who you choose to be.

The story of Wim the convert

Solutions to spiritual predicaments aren't exclusively religious in nature; we are multifaceted beings with body, mind, soul. Now, allow me to share the story of Wim, a convert.

Upon embracing Islam, Wim heard of the merits of memorising the Quran. However, after several weeks of struggling to commit it to memory, he turned to his local imam for guidance. The imam attributed his weak memory to sin and cited Imam Shāfiʿī's famous words

> Knowledge is light and Divine light is not given to the sinner!

The imam also told Wim that the Prophet of Allah (peace be upon him) said that Allah said,

> And for some of My servants, not knowing is better, and if I would have given them knowledge, then they would have turned into disbelievers![4]

Wim, eager and attentive, grew anxious. He asked the imam for a solution. The imam advised him to repent and seek forgiveness from Allah. But Wim, a recent convert, struggled to identify his sins. Still, he repented devoutly for a whole week to no avail.

Wim was disheartened, convinced that memorising the Quran

---

[4] *Tareekh ibn ʿAsakir, al Bayhaqi in (al Asma), Ibn Abi Dunya in (al Awliya), Ibn Rajab in (Jami' al 'ulum wal ḥikam). The meaning is correct, the authenticity of the the sanad disputable.*

could cast him into Hell. His joy faded, and he withdrew into his thoughts, much to his mother's concern. He abandoned his pastimes and former cheerfulness. Was this the same Wim who used to make others laugh and feel good?

His mother, deeply worried, urged him to see a doctor, sensing something was wrong. After conducting blood tests, the doctor diagnosed a deficiency in iron, magnesium, and a need for Vitamin B, and Omega 3 and 9. The doctor explained that these deficiencies likely impaired his concentration, hindering Quranic memorisation.

Six weeks later, with treatment adhered to, Wim's struggles persisted. The doctor explained the complexity of nature and nurture, genetics, and DNA, suggesting that memorisation might not align with everyone's strengths and that understanding the text was more important than memorising it.[5]

This disheartened Wim. Was it because of divine predestination or genes? Once a star student, Wim now sat isolated, wrestling with questions about the world, divine justice, heaven, hell, sin, and human limitations.

The school psychologist, noticing a change in Wim's demeanour, asked to speak with him during a break. Creating a safe space, she encouraged Wim to share his concerns, delving into his past and uncovering the impact of his stepmother who had undermined his self-esteem since his parents' divorce.

Despite months of intervention by the psychologist to rid Wim of

---

[5] *More about this in my book: Memorising the Holy Scripture; Why, Who, How?*

the self-doubt that supposedly impeded his memory, Wim's Quranic memorisation did not improve. The psychologist then suggested that memorisation might not align with his unique capacities and encouraged him to adapt his dreams to suit his abilities and be at peace with his limitations.

All these experts were correct according to their perspective yet were incomplete. We are not merely souls, neither are we solely minds nor solely bodies. We encompass all these aspects; we are humans. Our multidimensional nature defines us. Neglecting any aspect of our being can lead to detrimental consequences on our journey towards spiritual enlightenment and religious empowerment.

"Game over!" Wim muttered to himself, feeling overwhelmed. "It's all because of my sins, my genes, and my stepmother. But if everything is decreed by the Divine, then the fact that I have these genes and that my father married such a difficult woman must also be part of His decree. Why though? If I didn't know better, I might have started to doubt Allah. It just doesn't seem fair to lead a life that will eventually prevent me from becoming a *ḥāfiẓ* of the divine book."

Wim returned home; his heart heavy. But as he browsed the internet, something extraordinary caught his eye: an ad that boldly proclaimed, "Memorise the Quran in 18 months!" With newfound determination, Wim rushed out of his house, not even bothering to grab his jacket. The rain poured down relentlessly, but he paid no attention. He ran to the nearby Islamic Centre.

Upon his arrival, the director of the centre was alarmed by Wim's apparent distress and asked, "What's wrong, Wim? How can I assist you?" Drenched but determined, Wim blurted out, "I want to memorise the Quran!" The director, intrigued by Wim's urgency, inquired about his story.

With unwavering enthusiasm, Wim opened a small booklet of Juz' 'Amma. It was written in a phonetic script with curious markings beneath and above specific letters. To Wim, it all seemed overwhelmingly complicated to memorise. However, the director, wearing a reassuring smile, offered a clear roadmap, "My dear Wim, to commit the Quran to memory, you need just two things: a knowledgeable teacher and the ability to read Arabic. Once you master these, you'll become a *ḥāfiẓ*!"

Wim felt an overwhelming sense of joy. It was so profound that when he encountered the imam, the doctor, and the psychologist later, they all inquired about what had happened. Wim decided to keep his newfound hope to himself, recognising that they had all provided valuable insights, albeit from their distinct perspectives. He understood that the real solution to his religious predicament wasn't solely religious, medical, nor psychological; it was fundamentally holistic.

As to whether Wim ultimately achieved the status of a *ḥāfiẓ*, that's a story left to your imagination. What is certain, though, is that he is no longer confined to his room, gazing at the walls, trying to make sense of the world. He is likely out there, sharing his incredible journey with others!

Solutions to religious problems

People often assume that the solution to their spiritual dilemmas lies solely within the realm of religion. I do not shy away from saying that often, these issues are not exclusively religious. We are complex beings, not just souls. We encompass the mind, body, and the soul, navigating the intricacies of relationships, finances, work, family... Amid all this, it's easy to lose sight of the present moment.

When my clients seek guidance regarding anger issues, I opt for a nuanced approach rather than relying solely on conventional advice. Rather than offering direct quotations from hadith—despite their profound wisdom imparted by our revered Prophet Muhammad (peace be upon him)—I delve deeper into the context. It's crucial to recognise that the Prophet addressed specific cases where anger emanated from inherent character traits, rather than being solely influenced by external factors.

Misguided individuals often push people into despair when they oversimplify the problem. They may admonish someone with anger issues to fear Allah or remind them of Allah's anger. This advice mirrors the wisdom of the great Imam al-Ghazali. However, such counsel is effective when one can control their anger, not when one is controlled by their anger due to underlying factors.

I could spend years reminding someone about Allah's anger and extolling the virtues of patience and humility, but what if their anger is rooted in something entirely different?

There is always an underlying cause, which can be spiritual, like arrogance, envy, jealousy, or it can be psychological, such as narcissism, an inferiority complex, anxiety, depression, stress, or grief. Let's not forget that physical conditions like diabetes, high blood pressure, insomnia, or even hormonal fluctuations can trigger anger.

When Allah praises those who control their anger in surah Āl-ʿImrān,[6] it's a prompt for us to investigate the root cause rather than merely seeking refuge in Allah, crucial as that may be. Inability to manage one's anger is not necessarily a sign of a lack of awe for Allah or disrespect for the message of the Prophet Muhammad (peace be upon him). This is why religious leaders should be more than memorisers of texts.

Consider how many struggling believers with a fading spiritual connection and a religious burnout go untreated due to the misconception that solutions for religious and spiritual issues must exclusively be religious and spiritual. And by the way; what does 'religious' really mean?

Prophet Mohammed (peace be upon him) said:

> "There is nothing wrong with healing methods as long as they do not contain shirk."[7]

---

[6] "Hurry towards your Lord's forgiveness and a Garden as wide as the heavens and earth prepared for the righteous, who give, both in prosperity and adversity, who restrain their anger and pardon people. God loves those do good." [Q3:133-4]
[7] *Sahih Ibn Hibban: c0S4*

An example of the prophet's (peace be upon him) psychological approach

Let me share a story that might astonish you about a man who approached the Prophet Muhammad (peace be upon him_ and publicly said, "Allow me to commit adultery." Imagine someone walking into a mosque and shouting at the imam, "Allow me to fornicate!"

Proximity Control, Self-Examination, and Privacy

The Prophet Muhammad asked the man to come closer[8] and repeat what he had said. This approach has a psychological dimension. When you ask someone to reiterate their statement, they listen to themselves, promoting self-awareness and prompting them to question the validity of their thoughts.[9] Additionally, requesting the man to come closer indicates that such matters should be discussed privately, in a safe and non-judgmental space.

Inviting perspective-taking

The Prophet then engaged the man in a series of questions, asking whether he would like such actions to happen to his family members. By putting the man in the shoes of those affected, he induced empathy and understanding. We call this 'inviting

---

[8] In Islamic psychotherapy, we refer to inviting someone to draw nearer and soften their speech as "adjusting physical closeness and vocal demeanour," or "modulating proximity and tone." The intention behind this practice is to achieve specific goals: (a) fostering a sense of privacy, (b) nurturing intimacy and connection, (c) promoting comfort and reassurance, and (d) alleviating anxiety.

[9] In Islamic counselling, we refer to this practice as "tadabbur al-nafs" or "muhasabah," which translates to self-reflection or self-examination. This technique encourages the client to vocalise their thoughts and feelings, facilitating a deeper understanding of their inner world. By articulating their emotions and concerns, individuals can gain heightened self- awareness and insight. While it may not have a specific technical term, it closely aligns with the principles of self-reflection and self-awareness emphasised in Islamic counselling and therapy.

perspective-taking' in psychology.[10]

Religious and spiritual counselling

Following this interaction, the Prophet placed his hand on the man's head and made a heartfelt supplication for his forgiveness, purification, and protection from sin.[11] As the narrator Abū Umāma recalls, the young man never looked or lusted after anything prohibited again.

The Prophet Muhammad could have taken a different route, one that aligns with our modern 'religious' standards, and limit himself to supplicating for the young man. But since his supplications are always answered, he sought to teach us how we can deal with such situations. He understood that not everyone can rely solely on prayer. While supplications hold great importance, he taught us to:

"Tie your camel and trust in Allah."[12]

His approach was a psychological one, invoking empathy and placing himself in the other person's shoes to facilitate behavioural change.

Our Creator blessed us with the beautiful gift of empathy, allowing us to better understand one another. Thus, when Mohammed (peace be upon him) completed his 'counselling' session, he made a heartfelt supplication. This was the therapeutic goal; by voicing the supplication aloud, he imprinted

---

[10] *Inviting perspective-taking is a communication technique that encourages individuals to consider and understand the viewpoints of others. This is achieved by asking open-ended questions, actively listening to their responses, and using reflective statements to acknowledge their feelings. The goal is to foster empathy, promote understanding, and enhance communication in various contexts, including conflict resolution and relationship building.*

[11] *The combination of counselling and supplication is a practiced in faith-based counselling or spiritual counselling.*

[12] *Tirmidhī: h.2517, Ibn Ḥibbān: h.731*

a new way of thinking in the mind of his companion.[13]

This example was very clear. However, you can easily understand why countless individuals are left untreated; their imams or scholars are looking in the wrong direction.

---

[13] *The entire story shows us the reality of spiritual restoration or spiritual intervention. It has everything to do with helping a person to acknowledge their wrongdoing and reconciliate with his-her Lord. Although spiritual restoration is found in Christian midst, the form, shape and reality differ within Muslim circles.*

Four Kinds of People in Relation to Mental Health and Spiritual Problems

Today, we observe four distinct types of people within the Muslim community in relation to mental health and providing solutions to spiritual problems:

1. Experts in Mental Health Without a Traditional Background

These individuals work outside the boundaries of Islamic teachings and are typically unaware of ancient Muslim writings on the topic. While their love for Allah and His Messenger is not being unquestioned, their understanding of Islam is limited. They often confide in me that their lack of Islamic insight causes them to doubt whether they should be treating Muslims from a religious perspective.

2. Experts in Islamic Sciences without any understanding of Mental Health

Some may even hold a negative opinion of mental health, possibly considering it, at the very least, disliked, as clients/patients must 'expose' their weaknesses—and potentially sins—on their path to healing.

These scholars feel compelled to share their opinion simply because it's a trending topic. Individuals without expertise should remain silent about subjects beyond their grasp.

3. Traditionally Educated Individuals with Basic Knowledge of Mental Health

These individuals are experts in one area and possess a solid foundation in the other. This combination - of basic knowledge in one science and mastery of the other - is sufficient for providing Islamic counselling and therapy for Muslims.

4. Mental Health Experts with Basic Knowledge of Islamic Sciences

Final Remarks

Solutions to spiritual problems are not always spiritual ones. They can also be physical, mental, and emotional solutions. Failing to acknowledge that we are more than just a soul, just a mind, or just a body leads to numerous complications on your path to spiritual enlightenment and religious growth.

What is Repentance?

This section seeks to awaken a kind of repentance that goes beyond the mere apology, "Sorry, I will never do it again, I promise!" Instead, it encourages you to delve deeper and explore the profound reality of repentance. Only when you understand this deeper essence will you genuinely desire and seek true repentance.

At its core, repentance is:

- The act of returning to Allah after having forsaken Him.
- The realisation that love should never be met with rebellion.
- The heartfelt plea to the One you have 'wronged' to open His doors for you once more; doors that you willingly and knowingly closed behind you, unsure if He would ever welcome you back into His presence.

Repentance is born from a wounded heart that feels unable to go on without its Lord.

Think of sin as creating a barrier between you and the Almighty. On the other hand, repentance is tearing down that wall and finding your way back to Him. Often, those who are lost in sin are unaware of their state because their hearts have become hardened, their eyes blinded, their ears deafened, and their tongues muted. They can't see the path back to Allah or even hear His call:

> "They are wilfully deaf, dumb, and blind, so they will never return to the Right Path."(Q2:18)

> "They forgot about Allah, so He made them forget their share." (Q9:67)

Repentance is returning to the very purpose for which you were created; it is about reconciliation with your true self. Some have described repentance as nothing less than "Allah giving you a new heart to love Him with, without hindrance."

It is a Divine act, performed within the believer by the Almighty Himself:

> "And Allah has also turned in mercy to the three who had remained behind, whose guilt distressed them until the earth, despite its vastness, seemed to close in on them, and their souls were torn in anguish. They knew there was no refuge from Allah except in Him. Then He turned to them with *tawba* (repentance) so that they might repent. Surely Allah alone is the Accepter of Repentance, Most Merciful." (Q 9:118)

This verse reveals that He inspired them to repent because He had chosen to forgive them even before their repentance! He is the One who brings His servant back to Him:

> "Whoever Allah wills to guide, He opens their heart to Islam. But whoever He wills to lead astray, He makes their chest tight and constricted as if they were climbing up into the sky. This is how Allah dooms those who disbelieve." (Q6:125)

The essence of repentance lies in understanding that it has little to do with you and everything to do with the Almighty. He Who chooses to bless you with a new beginning. He Who creates the desire to repent within your heart. This is what the name al-Tawwāb signifies. Ibn al Qayyim described al-Tawwāb as the One who invites us to repentance and inserts the desire for Allah's forgiveness into the hearts of man.

وَكَذَلِكَ التَّوَّابُ مِنْ أَوْصَافِهِ

وَالتَّوْبُ فِي أَوْصَافِهِ نَوْعَانِ

إِذْنٌ بِتَوْبَةِ عَبْدِهِ وَقَبُولُهَا

بَعْدَ المَتَابِ بِمِنَّةِ المَنَّانِ

And accepting forgiveness is also one of His characteristics. Repentance is of two kinds: The permission He grants the servant to repent and accepting his repentance after repenting; such is the favour of the Bestower of favours.[14]

Repentance is the act of fleeing from the ego and Satan towards Allah alone. It involves forsaking sin because you love Allah more than yourself. It is not motivated by fear of others' opinions nor is it the coincidence of being barred from that sin. Repentance is the repentance of hearts. It is closely tied to detesting sin knowing

---

[14] *Madarij as Salikeen: V.1, P.312.* it is important to note that tawwāb is on the morphological pattern of fa"al فَعَّال . This pattern is used for: (a) the doer of something, (b) emphasising on something (hyperbole), (c) Indicating a large quantity of something. In light of the former it means that Allah is the One doing tawba, meaning He guides to forgiveness and grants forgiveness, and He does this often and a lot. If it does show something, than it is definitely the importance of knowing the Arabic language.

that sin lies at the root of estrangement from Allah and spiritual decay.

> And that he hates, dislikes, despises to return to disbelief (and sin and ingratitude) after Allah saved him from it, as strongly as he would dislike being thrown into Hell on Judgment Day.[15]

True repentance is never returning to sin. It is a turning point, a rebirth:

> Is he who was dead and whom We revived and provided a light to live with among people equal to he who resides in obscurity and finds no way out? (Quran, 6:122)

Repentance is freeing yourself from deviant desires to reconnect with Him. It has everything to do with forsaking sin because you are yearning for His love. Repentance answers the call of a suffering soul in rebellion against a dark past. It is about constructing a fortress around your life, changing your ways, and building watchtowers to keep the enemy at bay. It is about exchanging a deviant desire for a legitimate one. Repentance is fleeing from Allah's anger and the oppression of the self, turning to none but Him.

Whenever you repent, regardless of how insignificant it may seem to you, it is nothing less than a divine invitation. It is essential not to dwell on your sin nor on your low self-esteem. When you utter words of forgiveness, you are only allowed to

---

[15] *Ṣaḥīḥ al-Bukhārī*, 21

utter them because you are forgiven. This is because His wanting to forgive you precedes you begging for forgiveness. Your begging for forgiveness is indicating that He wants to forgive. This is because if He did not want to forgive, you would not have asked for His forgiveness. Satan seeks to make you doubt Allah's mercy, and your conscience may consume you until you are left with nothing but the bones of guilt. To break free from this, believe in Him as He has described Himself, even if it does not always align with your thoughts or feelings.

> "Flee towards Allah!" (Q51:50)

In this divine verse, Allah doesn't specify where to fly from but rather Who to fly to. Flee from all that veers you away from His divine presence, for sin has never served as a pathway to the Almighty. When panic sets in, the imperative is action, not contemplation. In moments of dire urgency, one acts on instinct. Flee not to escape, but to seek refuge.

Repentance is the safeguard of your immortal essence, a journey towards redemption. It demands liberation from the shackles of transgression, a cleansing of the innermost sanctum of the soul. For His gaze penetrates beyond mere outward appearances, delving into the recesses of the spirit.

> He does not look at your bodies or your features or your wealth. Rather, He looks at your hearts and deeds.".[16]

---

[16] Ṣaḥīḥ Muslim, h.6564

Genuine repentance

Genuine repentance is marked by an unwavering commitment to never return to the sinful path.

> O believers! Turn to Allah in (*naṣūḥ*) repentance, so your Lord may absolve you of your sins and admit you into Gardens, under which rivers flow, on the Day Allah will not disgrace the Prophet or the believers with him. Their light will shine ahead of them and on their right. They will say, 'Our Lord! Perfect our light for us and forgive us. For You are truly Most Capable of everything.' (Quran, 66:8)

It is, in essence, to repent and sever ties with the sin, to renounce it for eternity. However, it is a Herculean task when the root cause of sin remains obscure. Sin, you see, is merely a symptom of a wounded spirit, a frail body, or an ailing mind. Sin is a plea for help or a form of self-inflicted suffering. One who reverts to sin has not experienced true repentance. Genuine repentance ushers in a spiritual awakening, making one vigilant against the snares of the Devil.

When you fall into the same sin, you must acknowledge that true repentance has eluded you, as your efforts were but a fleeting endeavour.

Blossoming of True Repentance

True repentance only blossoms when it brings about an enduring transformation, when the heart recoils from what Allah abhors. Scholars have said that repentance happens when you are prepared to trade forbidden desires for permissible ones. Others claim that it is the outcome of realising Allah's displeasure with the sinner.

Do not despair, for no sin is beyond forgiveness. This is why we must always hold onto hope. No matter how big our mistakes, there is always a way back to Allah's mercy. The story of Adam illustrates this. Even after he was expelled from Paradise, he was given a special supplication to find his way back to Allah and the Gardens of Eden. His story reminds us that no matter what we have done, there is always a way back to Him.

> Then Adam was inspired with words of prayer by his Lord, so He accepted his repentance. Surely, He is the Accepter of Repentance, Most Merciful. (Quran, 2:37)

These were the words Allah inspired Adam and his wife Eve with:

> They replied, "Our Lord! We have wronged ourselves. If You do not forgive us and have mercy on us, we will certainly be losers. (Quran, 7:23)

> Is he who was dead and whom we revived and provided a light to live with among people equal to he who resides in obscurity and finds no way out? (Quran, 6:122)

Repentance is freeing yourself from deviant desires to connect with Him, and it has everything to do with forsaking sin because you are desperately seeking His love. Sinning literally destroys your true self.

Repentance, on the other hand, is the opposite. It is answering the Divine call to live a happy and balanced life in this world and a beautiful one in the next.

> "O believers, answer Allah and His Prophets' call when they call you to that which gives you life!" (Quran, 8:24)

The journey back to the Almighty is a quest for His closeness, an embrace within His divine presence. Loneliness—life without Allah—is a heavy burden on the soul. It entangles the sinner in profound grief. It is an emotional storm where nothing else matters. Even if the world's treasures were laid at the sinner's feet, happiness would still elude him, covered by the dark cloud of sorrow that veils his heart.

Imagine this: You suffer the devastating loss of a child, and on the same day, you receive a significant bonus at work. Although the bonus would bring happiness, the profound sorrow of losing your child overshadows any joy you might feel. This is akin to the experience of those who once felt a deep connection with Allah. No matter what worldly achievements they attain, nothing compares to the joy of being close to Him and basking in His love. His presence surpasses all earthly pleasures and accomplishments.

Repentance marks the first step toward Allah after turning away from Him. It is returning to the One who cared for you, watched over you, and One who you could always trust.

Ibn 'Aṭā' Allah tells us that expecting divine goodness in return for what you "give" leads to despair, while recognising the continuous love bestowed upon you, regardless of your actions, opens the door to hope.

Repentance isn't just a spiritual state (*maqām*); it's a spiritual fortress within you. Unlike a temporary spiritual abode (*ḥāl*), a *maqām* endures within, a constant reminder of the journey back to the Almighty, where hope comes forth from His unwavering love.

Hence Ibn al Qayyim (may Allah be pleased with him) said:

> "Repentance is the beginning, the centre, and the end of the path."[17]

In summary:

Grasping the essence of repentance serves as the initial stride in reconciling with the Almighty. The reality of repentance extends beyond mere words; it is about eliminating every barrier that separates you from His love and steering clear of what provokes His displeasure.

Repentance, in its truest form, is a transformative journey aimed at fostering a closer connection with the Divine, removing obstacles on your path toward Him, and invoking His mercy.

---

[17] Madarij as- salikeen

Feeling guilty

Imperfection is part of being human; we all make mistakes. Thinking we can reach Paradise by being flawless is just a fantasy.[18] Only Allah is truly perfect. As believers, we strive to get better without letting ourselves fall into despair. Allah's mercy is vast and never-ending, giving us hope even when we make mistakes.

In my capacity as a religious counsellor, I often encounter souls filled with a deep longing for self-improvement. Their beauty lies in their earnest desire to rid themselves of what they deem unworthy within. Yet, many struggle with uncertainty regarding the transformative journey—how to embark upon it and what it demands. Some find themselves trapped in a cycle of self-condemnation for addictions, shortcomings, imperfections, mistakes, and sins. It's paramount to grasp that recognising a sin should stir remorse, leading one towards constructive self-examination, mindfulness, and enduring transformation.

---

[18] *"Your deeds will not be the reason for you to enter Paradise!" Not even you, Messenger of Allah? "Not even me!"(Saheeh al Bukhari) "Each child of Adam is a sinner. The best among sinners are they who repent." (Ahmad, at Tirmidhi, Ibn Majah)*

No mention of 'guilt' in Quran and Sunna

Notably, the absence of the word 'guilt' in the Quran and Sunna is significant.[19] Guilt, often tied to one's conscience, emerges when our actions conflict with our deeply held values, functioning on a cognitive level. From a spiritual perspective, this feeling of guilt can be counterproductive. The burden of guilt has, unfortunately, driven some Muslims towards depression, eroding their self-esteem and fostering thoughts of self-harm.

This underlying distress stems from a belief that Allah has abandoned them, questioning therefore the value of their lives. In these moments, individuals may resemble nihilists, losing all sense of meaning, or existentialists, fervently seeking purpose but struggling to find a genuine one. It's crucial to navigate this complex terrain with an understanding that Allah's mercy is ever-present, guiding us towards redemption rather than despair.

The ache of feeling forsaken by the Divine is akin to the turmoil of those navigating a divorce or breakup. It's a profound attachment

---

[19] *Guilt is a complex emotion that arises when a person believes they have done something wrong or violated their own moral code. It can have various underlying causes and manifestations. Let's break down some common types of guilt:*

Objective Guilt: *This is a type of guilt that is based on an actual violation of ethical or moral standards. It's the result of a person knowingly engaging in a behavior that is considered wrong by societal or personal standards.*

Subjective Guilt: *This form of guilt is based on a person's perception of their actions, even if those actions don't objectively warrant guilt. It might occur when someone feels guilty for things they shouldn't, often due to high personal standards or an overly self-critical nature.* **Survivor's Guilt:** *This is a specific type of guilt experienced by individuals who have survived a traumatic event that others did not. They might feel guilty for having survived when others did not, even if they had no control over the situation.*

Parental Guilt: *Parents might feel guilty for not being able to meet their own expectations of perfect parenting or for making decisions that they believe have negatively impacted their children.*

Reactive Guilt: *(Remorse): This type of guilt arises in response to a specific event or situation where a person's actions or choices have caused harm to someone else. It's often characterised by regret, sorrow, and a desire to make amends.*

severed, a sanctuary shattered, and hearts left adrift without refuge.

Ironically, it's often the devout souls, immersed in spirituality, who find themselves balancing on the edge of despair. Their love for Allah is not just a facet of their existence but their *raison d'être* (reason to be). Being loved by Him is their greatest wish.

Those who callously dispense afflictions upon the hearts of believers, injecting them with the venom of despair, must be corrected. Their actions throw genuine believers into the depths of spiritual and emotional agony.

> "O Mohammed, why did you make my servants despair? Go back to them and make them laugh, like you made them cry!"[20]

These individuals, by their actions and words, inscribe onto the hearts of sinners the distressing idea that they are devoid of love and unworthy of affection. This perception leads to a belief that Allah has forsaken them, with the bleak prospect of Hell as their inevitable fate.

Such an approach deeply troubles me, as it suggests a profound misunderstanding of divine compassion. The narrative they propagate paints a dark picture, overshadowing the inherent mercy and love that Allah offers to all, regardless of their perceived shortcomings.

As I contemplate the roots of our despair, I wonder if our

---

[20] al Adab al Mufrad, al Bukhari h.254

distorted perception of Allah lies at its core. Belief in the Divine should never result in despair or a sense of emptiness. Our understanding of sin and the motivations driving us to commit them has become warped, leading us to lose faith in the possibility of change and branding ourselves as "failures" and "worthless."

To you, the seeker of truth, I urge: do not let guilt consume your soul. It is merely a shadow cast by your ego. Your sins do not harm the Divine, but they do inflict wounds upon the very sanctuary of your being.

Recognise that guilt is an ego-driven emotion, rooted in the fear of consequences. True repentance, however, is a pilgrimage back to the embrace of Allah. It is acknowledging your flaws and turning your spirit towards the light. Let your remorse be a guiding force, not to flee guilt, but to mend your soul and reunite with the infinitely merciful One.

The Origin of Sin

It's crucial to emphasise that the root of sin isn't always inherently malicious or driven by malevolence; more often, it stems from yielding to our natural impulses in ways contrary to the teachings of Allah. Our very creation and the complex workings of our minds play a pivotal role in our inclining towards sinful behaviour.

The impulse to sin is often nothing but a manifestation of our primal urge for survival. Essentially, our physical selves serve as survival mechanisms, propelled by fundamental desires for wealth and health, reproduction, and self-preservation. We meticulously analyse our environment to secure our position within society.

The inclination to seek visibility, affection, power, reverence, followership, affluence, and renown traces back to an evolutionary impulse rooted in the quest for survival. This fundamental drive is deeply ingrained within our psyche and shapes our interactions with the world around us.

Psychologists, with their nuanced understanding of human behaviour, often collaborate with businesses and corporations to leverage and capitalise on these basic emotions. They recognise that at the heart of our actions lies a deep-seated fear of exclusion, mediocrity, and unnoticed—a fear that compels us to strive for recognition and success.[21]

---

[21] Marketing profoundly taps into our survival instincts, particularly the fight or flight response. This ancient mechanism, deeply embedded in our biology, prepares us to respond to threats with swift action. Fear-based advertising leverages this instinct by creating urgency, compelling us to act quickly to avoid perceived dangers. For instance, public health campaigns use fear to highlight the risks of smoking or drunk driving, urging immediate behavioural changes to ensure our safety.

Our brain orchestrates an array of functions, transmitting messages to our body, evoking emotions, and culminating in

---

Navigating Defense Mechanisms

Defense mechanisms are psychological strategies we unconsciously use to protect ourselves from anxiety and distress. These include denial, repression, and rationalisation. Marketers skilfully exploit these mechanisms by presenting products in ways that allow us to avoid unpleasant truths or justify our desires. For example, luxury brands use aspirational marketing to help us rationalise extravagant purchases as symbols of success and self- improvement, rather than mere indulgence.

Engaging Basic Emotions

Emotions are the core drivers of our decision-making processes. Douglas Van Praet emphasises that emotions are not barriers to rational thought but the foundation upon which our decisions are built. Marketers harness this insight by creating emotionally charged campaigns that evoke happiness, sadness, fear, and anger. Emotional advertising is incredibly powerful because it creates lasting impressions and influences our behaviour more deeply than logical appeals.

1. Happiness: Advertisements that evoke happiness, such as those featuring joyful moments or heartwarming stories, enhance brand perception and foster loyalty. Positive emotions increase sharing and engagement, making the message more memorable and impactful.

2. Sadness: Campaigns that trigger empathy and sadness can forge deep emotional connections. For instance, stories of personal struggle or adversity often led to greater empathy and support for a brand or cause.

3. Fear: Fear-based marketing creates urgency, prompting immediate action. This tactic is common in health and safety campaigns, where the goal is to highlight dangers and encourage preventive measures.

4. Anger: While risky, anger can motivate action. Advertisements that provoke anger about social injustices or environmental issues can galvanise viewers to support a cause or take action.

The Essence of Emotional Marketing

Marketing strategies are deeply intertwined with our basic human instincts and emotions. By understanding and leveraging these psychological and physiological responses, marketers can craft campaigns that resonate on a fundamental level. This approach not only drives consumer behaviour but also builds stronger, more emotional connections with brands. Understanding these connections helps us see how every element of marketing serves a greater purpose in influencing and shaping our decisions, ultimately guiding us toward products and services that resonate with our deepest needs and desires.

actions that, if not guided by *fiṭra* (natural disposition), might ultimately manifest as what we refer to as sin.[22]

The distinction between a good deed and a bad one often lies not in the deed itself, but in the manner of its execution.

Prophet Mohammed (peace be upon him) conveyed,

> "And you are rewarded for being intimate." When asked if one would be rewarded for restraining sexual desires, the Prophet replied, "Yes. If one were to still his sexual desire in an illegitimate manner, would he not be sinning? Similarly, when he extinguishes his sexual lust, he will be rewarded"[23]

Imam al-Ghazālī clarified that a sin is either an excess or a lack of certain emotions, instincts, or physical inclinations. One should not become angry for the sake of one's ego, but anger for the sake of truth and justice is praiseworthy.

Understanding this perspective facilitates a more compassionate judgement of sinners. It allows us to recognise that a sinner is not

---

[22] **Hypothalamus:** Regulates hunger, thirst, temperature, and sexual behaviour.
Amygdala: Processes emotions, fear, and aggression.
Basal Ganglia: Influences habits, motivation, and rewards.
Prefrontal Cortex: Handles decision-making and impulse control.
Brainstem: Controls vital functions like heart rate and breathing.
Nucleus Accumbens: Part of the reward system for pleasurable experiences.
These regions collaborate to drive various survival-related behaviours and emotional responses. Not knowing how to temper and tame these drives and not understanding – even at a lower level – how the brain and the body work together can cause more harm than good: "And in your own selves are signs, do you not see?!" (Quran, 51:21)

[23] Muslim, h.1006

inherently evil; rather, they may be unaware of Allah's prohibitions due to ignorance or a lack of guidance on controlling their urges and desires. This discussion specifically pertains to sins that do not involve harming others, as such actions contravene the moral compass bestowed upon mankind by Allah.

Allah wired us to love wealth, marriage, intimacy, and having children. The innate hunger for more—protection, status, wealth, and food—is not inherently sinful. However, our culpability lies in the paths we choose to attain these pursuits.

> The enjoyment of worldly desires—women, children, treasure of gold and silver, fine horses, cattle, and fertile land—has been made appealing to people. These are the pleasures of this worldly life, but with Allah is the finest destination. (Quran, 3:14)

> Wealth and children are the adornment of this worldly life, but the everlasting good deeds are far better with your Lord in reward and in hope. (Quran, 18:46)

> Ask, O Prophet, "Who has forbidden the adornments and lawful provisions Allah has brought forth for His servants?" Say, "They are for the enjoyment of the believers in this worldly life, but they will be exclusively theirs on the Day of Judgment. This is how We make Our revelations clear for people of knowledge. (Quran, 7:32)

The root cause of sin often stems not from a deliberate desire to rebel but rather from a physical impulse that one struggles to tame, channel, and direct.

Once Upon a Time When Humans Didn't Sin

Once, many millennia ago, you and I harboured no desire other than to be in the exclusive company of Allah, free from wants and needs. Since the dawn of time, Allah desired to be worshipped by physical beings who, through effort and out of their free will, sought His pleasure by resisting their physical drives and desires.

> The Jinn were created from smokeless fire, and the angels from radiant, transparent light.[24]

We were souls—untarnished, pure, angelic. Three, intangible entities inhabited the world of souls: souls, *jinn*, and angels. One of them was destined to inhabit a tangible body. This entity would be tasked with disciplining that body, guiding it toward the Divine, galloping through the gardens of divine nearness, yearning to return to its origin, its Maker.

However, as soon as the soul descended into a body crafted specifically for her, she encountered the weight of this earthly vessel. No longer free to traverse the plains of divine nearness, she realised she was no longer a pure celestial being. She became tethered to this alien body, unfamiliar with its functions. To articulate her feelings, she had to learn to speak. To please her Lord she had to learn how to take control of this body, how to sit, walk, run, jump, roll, climb, pray, read, speak for the pleasure of her lord.

Over time, the soul and body became so entwined that distinguishing between the two proved challenging—they seemed inseparable. The soul, created to discipline this body, found itself

---

[24] Muslim

being taken over. Despite being designed to tame this body, the soul became tamed by it. It became disoriented, gradually forgetting its separateness. Simultaneously, the tangible body underwent physical, motor, sensory, and cognitive development, growing stronger day by day.[25] Throughout this process, the soul was not instructed on how to care for this body, how to tame it, nor how to strengthen it enough to direct it toward its Lord and Master.

This body was meant to serve the Lord. It was designed to overcome all obstacles and to be the representative of Allah on earth. Its design is so ingenious. It heals itself, protects itself, and makes its own choices. It is a true survival machine. Indeed, the intention is for the soul to inhabit it for as long as possible to worship its Lord. That is her test. There are no fallen angels in Islam, but there are fallen souls. Indeed, every soul was pure and immaculate until it allowed the body to guide it instead of taming the body and using this ingenious system to its advantage. The body is its armour and shield that transcends any form of nanotechnology.

The body outgrew the soul because the soul was neglected. But one day, when the soul hears that divine call–perhaps it will be a man in the street, a parent, a friend, an imam, a scholar, or a book reminding her of her existence and presence in this world–she felt alive and determined to continue on her everlasting journey to His Majesty.

> O believers! Respond to Allah and His Messenger when he calls you to that which

---

[25] *It went through phases: the sensorimotor phase (0-2), the preoperative phase (2-7), the operative phase (7-12) and then the formal-operative phase (12-...).*

> gives you life. And know that Allah stands between a person and their heart, and that to Him you will all be gathered. (Quran, 8:24)

The predicament arose when she found herself no longer in control. Weakened, she lay buried beneath the rubble of sin and the rocks of rebellion that the body, entrusted to her care, had amassed. Laden with guilt and sorrow, she transmitted her concerns to the brain, urging the dormant machine into action.

In this feeble state, she rekindled the cognitive and physical processes. The body responded by engaging in prayer, lowering its gaze. The once unrestrained tongue now adhered to truth, forsaking lies and harming others. By uttering apologies, arrogance found no place, and self-contempt evaporated. The soul felt a renewed sense of vitality. Its happiness radiated through the very body it inhabited, a testament to the transformative power of reawakening.

> "The sign of brightness can be seen on their faces from the trace of prostrating in prayer" (Quran, 48:49)

The reawakened soul

> Can those who had been dead, to whom We gave life and a light with which they can walk among people, be compared to those in complete darkness from which they can never emerge?[1] That is how the misdeeds of the disbelievers have been made appealing to them. (Quran, 6:122)

> The example of the one who celebrates the Praises of his Lord (Allah) in comparison to the one who does not celebrate the Praises of his Lord, is that of a living creature compared to a dead one.[26]

Yet, her premature celebration of victory proved to be unfounded. She discovered that relinquishing full control over the body led to her own suffering. It dawned on her that the body was not the sole determinant of her spiritual well-being. Thoughts, life experiences, traumas, financial struggles, emotions, and the environment all exerted direct influence on her essence. She realised that with her presence eternal happiness stood; without her, it crumbled.

Understanding the imperative to safeguard herself, she acknowledged the need to tend to all these varied dimensions. It became a duty for her to strive for holistic happiness, requiring a delicate balance, structure, and health in every aspect of her existence. In this pursuit, the soul recognised that many kindred souls remained entombed, awaiting liberation like caged birds.

---

[26] *Sahih al-Bukhari: h. 407, Sahih Muslim: h. 77*

Unfortunately, the call goes unheard, drowned amidst the excessive nourishment of our carnal selves, while insufficient attention is paid to the needs of our neglected souls.

My friend, this is your tale. You are the ancient soul navigating this alien vessel. The reins of mastery are in your grasp because, unequivocally, you are appointed as its custodian. It is your responsibility to steer and mould this earthly existence, fully acknowledging the gravity that comes with being the rightful custodian. Embrace the role of master, for within you lies the key to unlock the true potential of this intricate fusion of soul and body.

Summary

- The root of sin lies in an untamed body, unguided by the soul.
- Sin, fundamentally, is not inherently evil; rather, it often stems from the misdirection of natural drives or emotions.
- Achieving spiritual well-being necessitates a balanced emotional, financial, and social life.

Forgiving yourself

Forgiving yourself is crucial. Dwelling on past mistakes, faults, and sins is unhealthy. It doesn't mean belittling your sins, but rather, carrying on with life being conscious of the Almighty. To Him, we are what we are now, not what we were yesterday. Constant regret of the past will bring you down; beating yourself up today for actions five years ago hinders emotional healing and spiritual growth. In your own eyes, you'll always be that same person, preventing you from moving forward.

This is why forgiving yourself and believing in His forgiveness is paramount. He doesn't want you to linger in sorrow, isolating yourself from society due to lapses in abiding by His rules. His mercy surpasses your own mercy for yourself. He is *al-Raḥmān*, *al-Wadūd* (the Giver of love), *al-Laṭīf* (the Giver of gentleness), *al-Karīm* (the Generous), *al-Wahhāb* (the Bestower), *al-Jabbār* (the Healer of hearts). Repeat these names aloud; take an early morning walk in the park, listen to the birds, and say: "O *Raḥmān*, be merciful with me; O *Wadūd*, love me; O *Laṭīf*, be gentle with me; O *Karīm*, be generous to me; O *Wahhāb*, grant me; O *Jabbār*, heal me."

Sit on the grass, feel His love through the Universe He created for you. As the sun rises, heralding a new day, repeat these names. Breathe with the trees, the birds, the sky. Gradually, feel the warmth He bestows upon your heart; a genuine smile will appear. You sense it, don't you? He is there, beside you, healing you, watching over you, conveying without words that there's no need to be harsh with yourself. He forgives you before you seek forgiveness, just as He clothes you without being asked. He sustains you, inspires you, wakes you up every morning not to torment or punish you but to elevate your rank and immortalise your name.

The Danger of Closing the Door of Hope Upon Yourself

Shutting the door of hope upon yourself is profoundly harmful. Dwelling on your past is akin to a modern form of spiritual self-flagellation, which can lead to several detrimental effects.

Physical Harm

Repeated emotional self-flagellation can manifest in physical self-harm. When you constantly think the worst of yourself and believe that Allah has forsaken you, it can lead to physical manifestations of this inner turmoil. Spiritual self-harm can drive you to inflict physical pain upon yourself, seeking to atone for perceived sins or shortcomings in ways that are damaging and destructive.

Emotional and Physical Pain

Consistent self-inflicted emotional harm impacts your daily life, causing significant pain and discomfort. Activities like sleep, work, and even simple daily tasks become burdensome. Emotional pain can translate into physical symptoms, creating a cycle where the body and mind are in constant distress.

Psychological Distress

Spiritual self-flagellation induces overwhelming feelings of guilt, shame, and low self-esteem. This ongoing self-punishment contributes to negative self-perceptions, where you see yourself as unworthy or beyond redemption. Such distress can erode your mental health, leading to anxiety, depression, and a persistent sense of hopelessness.

Negative Emotional Impact

Emotional and spiritual self-flagellation intensifies feelings of anxiety, depression, and tendencies toward self-harm. It creates a vicious cycle of negative emotions that are hard to break. These emotions feed each other, deepening the sense of despair and isolation.

Distorted Beliefs

Distorted religious or spiritual beliefs that emphasise punishment and suffering can lead to an unhealthy relationship with your faith. Instead of experiencing the compassionate and merciful aspects of Allah, you might only see a punitive and harsh deity. This distortion prevents you from experiencing the true essence of spiritual growth and enlightenment.

Social Isolation

Emotional self-flagellation often leads to social isolation. You might hide your actions, feeling ashamed and fearing judgement. This isolation deprives you of the support and companionship that are crucial for healing and mental well-being. Without a support system, the path to recovery becomes even more challenging.

Normalising Pain

Self-inflicted emotional and physical pain can normalise the idea that pain is a valid coping mechanism. This dangerous belief leads to unhealthy responses to stress and an inability to manage emotions effectively. It creates a pattern where pain becomes the default reaction to any emotional disturbance.

Mental Health Risks

Prolonged self-flagellation poses serious risks to your mental health. It can lead to severe mental health issues, including chronic depression, anxiety disorders, and even suicidal thoughts. The continuous cycle of self-punishment prevents you from finding peace and healing.

Interference with Healing

Instead of promoting healing, self-flagellation hinders it. It distracts you from addressing the root causes of your distress, serving as a barrier to true emotional and spiritual recovery. By focusing on punishment rather than healing, you delay the process of becoming whole again.

Misunderstanding Religious Texts and Teachings

Emotional and spiritual self-flagellation often stems from a misinterpretation of religious teachings. Focusing on punitive measures rather than the intended spiritual growth leads to a warped understanding of your faith. It's essential to grasp that Allah's teachings are meant to guide you towards a fulfilling and compassionate life.

This underscores the importance of forgiving yourself! Embrace Allah's mercy and compassion and allow yourself the grace to heal and grow.

The Positive Impact of Forgiving Oneself on Well-Being

Forgiving oneself is a profound psychological process that influences various facets of well-being, encompassing emotions, thoughts, and even brain activity. Though the brain's response to self-forgiveness isn't fully comprehended, here's a simplified explanation of what forgiving oneself might do to the brain:

Emotional Relief

Forgiving yourself can alleviate stress and unease in your brain, providing a sense of emotional relief. Like a comforting embrace, self-forgiveness lightens the burden of guilt and self-blame. When you forgive yourself, it's as if a weight is being lifted, allowing certain parts of your brain to relax and find peace.

Positive Thinking

Self-forgiveness cultivates more positive thoughts. Your brain may shift its focus to the lessons learned from mistakes rather than dwelling on negative feelings. This shift in perspective fosters a happier and more hopeful state of mind. By embracing self-forgiveness, you open the door to growth and a brighter outlook on life.

Reward System

There's a specialised part of your brain that rewards positive actions or feelings. Forgiving yourself can activate this part, generating a sense of relief and satisfaction–a metaphorical pat on the back for being understanding and kind to yourself. This reward system reinforces the positive behaviour of self-compassion, encouraging you to continue on this path.

Stress Reduction

Guilt and self-blame induce significant stress in the brain. Self-forgiveness leads to a reduction in stress as you release negative feelings. This can have a soothing effect on your overall mood. By forgiving yourself, you create an environment within your mind that is conducive to peace and relaxation.

Brain Harmony

Optimal brain function occurs when thoughts and feelings are in harmony. Forgiving yourself contributes to aligning your thoughts with your emotions, fostering a sense of balance. This alignment promotes overall well-being, allowing you to navigate life with a clearer mind and a more settled heart.

Enhanced Self-Esteem

When you forgive yourself, you build a healthier self-image. Accepting your imperfections and recognising your efforts to improve contribute to a stronger sense of self-worth. This enhanced self-esteem empowers you to face challenges with confidence and resilience.

Improved Relationships

Self-forgiveness positively impacts your relationships with others. When you are kinder to yourself, it becomes easier to extend that kindness to those around you. This can lead to more meaningful and compassionate connections with family, friends, and community members.

Spiritual Growth

Embracing self-forgiveness aligns with the compassionate

teachings of Allah. It allows you to experience His mercy and love more fully. As you forgive yourself, you draw closer to Him, deepening your spiritual journey and finding greater fulfilment in your faith.

Increased Resilience

Forgiving yourself fosters resilience. It equips you with the emotional strength to bounce back from setbacks and challenges. With self-forgiveness, you develop a mindset that embraces growth and learning, enabling you to persevere through life's difficulties.

Remember, forgiving yourself is not about excusing past mistakes but about recognising your worth and embracing the opportunity to grow. By forgiving yourself, you open the door to a brighter, more fulfilling future, grounded in the mercy and love of Allah.

Inspired by al-Ghazali

In the quiet nooks of your heart's retreat, A battle brews, whispers bittersweet.
A wise old mystic now steps in,
as shadows part, let truths begin.

Unshackle chains of self-blame tight,
find comfort in Allah's forgiving light.
For He, the Merciful, understands,
The wobbles and fumbles of our human hands.

In every trip, a lesson's tucked,
In the darkest spots, there's still Divine luck. To mend the hurts, to soothe the soul, Seek His kindness

to make you whole.

Look back on the past with gentle cheer, let forgiveness whisper, "All is clear."

The sands of time, they ebb and flow, revealing paths where growth can show.

Oh, seeker of truth, let go the weight, Let Divine wisdom illuminate.

In seeking pardon, the soul finds rest, A journey towards the very best.

Between self-forgiveness and acknowledging the pain inflicted on others

Navigating the delicate relationship between self-forgiveness and acknowledging the pain inflicted on others is no easy task. But let's walk this path together, step by step.

First, take a moment to truly recognise the impact of your actions. Acknowledging this is your first step towards empathy and understanding the depth of the wounds you may have caused. It's not about dwelling on guilt, but about opening your heart to the experiences of others.

Begin the healing process with a sincere commitment to making amends. This means taking concrete steps to address the harm you've caused and seeking forgiveness from those affected. True remorse, paired with genuine efforts to make things right, forms the foundation of your journey towards transformation.

Remember, this journey won't be without its challenges. Emotions are complex, wounds can be deep, and not everyone will be ready to forgive immediately. Patience, humility, and a listening ear are your best allies here. Be prepared to meet these challenges with grace.

Cultivate compassion, both for yourself and for those you've impacted. Recognise that making mistakes is part of being human. Embrace the potential for growth and transformation that comes from facing and correcting your errors. This mindset will help you move forward with a lighter heart.

While self-forgiveness is crucial, it's equally important to take responsibility for your actions. Balance is key here. You need to heal yourself, but you also need to address the consequences of your actions on others.

Think of rebuilding trust as nurturing a delicate flower. It takes time and consistent care. Show sincerity and consistency in your actions as you work to rebuild trust. Understand that this process may be slow, and patience is essential.

Seek guidance along the way. Talk to trusted mentors, counsellors, or religious figures. Their insights can offer valuable perspectives and support, helping you find clarity on your path forward.

Ultimately, the journey to reconciliation involves navigating the difficult interplay of self-forgiveness, acknowledging the pain you've caused, and committing to healing. Approach this path with humility, sincerity, and a genuine desire to mend what has been broken.

Recognise that you're not alone in this journey. We all stumble and fall, but it's in getting up and striving to do better that we find our true strength. Trust in Allah's mercy, lean on the support of those around you, and believe in your capacity to grow and heal.

You've got this. Take each step with courage and faith, knowing that with every effort, you're moving closer to a place of peace and reconciliation.

Allah does not 'feed' on the suffering of His creation

For many years, I have traversed the landscapes of the Quran and Sunna, arriving at the conclusion that Allah and His Prophet never seek to dishearten the believers. They do not derive pleasure from the pain and grief of their followers. Instead, they beckon those who may have strayed from their covenant with Allah Almighty to return to the Master, the Majestic King. When Mohammed (peace be upon him) made people cry, Allah asked him: "Why did you lead My servants to despair? Go back to them and instill hope!"

Allah has no *schadenfreude*; He does not 'feed on' the suffering of His creation. The Prophet Muhammad, the earthly representative of Allah who applied the Quranic guidance, is described as:

> Concerned with your suffering, anxious for your well-being, and gracious and merciful to the believers (Quran, 9:128).

This leads me to believe that the sadomasochistic tendencies of humanity often manifest in words and minds, becoming embedded in the messages they share with their followers.

> Had We willed, We could have indeed shown them to you, O Prophet, and you would have surely recognised them by their appearance. But you will undoubtedly recognise them by their tone of speech. And Allah fully knows your deeds, O people. (Quran, 47:30).

Many preachers seem driven to evoke guilt, revelling in the success of making someone cry. They remain oblivious, or perhaps indifferent, to the multitude of seekers of Allah who, due to the impossibly high standards or the slamming shut of doors of hope, end up abandoning their pursuit of Allah. It is not a far-fetched notion for preachers, untrained by genuine spiritual guides (distinct from sectarian leaders), to be susceptible to spiritual maladies. Even at the culmination of their journey, it is the scholar and Quran-reciter who may find themselves cast into the depths of Hell.

Numerous individuals who outwardly project religious devotion often seek my counselling services. Their motivation stems from a sense that their inner selves—comprising thoughts, actions, dreams —do not align with the public persona they present. "It is an illusion to assume that people are immune to spiritual diseases, religious burnout, or personal flaws and mistakes only because they dress Islamically. "

Interestingly, I have discovered that individuals living in the mountains of Morocco or the deserts of Sudan, despite lacking literary prowess or social media presence, often embody profound religious authenticity. Their lives are a testament to the untold stories that should be shared.

It appears that many preachers struggle with a form of rankism, where individuals in positions of authority misuse their power to harm those they perceive as 'nobodies.' My interactions with students have uncovered valuable insights, indicating that spiritual growth isn't solely dependent on constant teaching. The complexity of human nature sometimes leads individuals to belittle others to fulfil their own need for superiority. This behaviour may be rooted in various factors.

Personal Hurt

Some preachers may project their own pain onto others, seeking validation or companionship in their suffering. By making others feel inferior, they may temporarily alleviate their own sense of inadequacy or misery.

Difficulty in Coping with Personal Pain

Preachers, like anyone else, may struggle with personal challenges or trauma. Difficulty in coping with their own pain may lead them to inadvertently inflict harm on others as a misguided attempt to cope or assert control.

Low Self-Esteem or Self-Confidence

Individuals with low self-esteem or low self-confidence may resort to belittling others to boost their own sense of worth or importance. By making others feel inferior, they may temporarily mask their own insecurities.

Subconscious Desire for Retribution

Some preachers may harbour subconscious desires for revenge or retribution, particularly if they have experienced harm or injustice themselves. They may unconsciously seek to assert power over others as a means of balancing perceived injustices.

Ignorance

Lack of understanding or awareness about Islamic teachings, spirituality, psychology, and mental health may contribute to harmful behaviour.

Preachers who are unaware of the deeper spiritual and

psychological dynamics may inadvertently perpetuate harmful attitudes or actions.

Summary

These factors shed light on why some Muslim preachers may engage in behaviours that undermine the spiritual growth and well-being of others. By recognising and addressing these underlying issues, we can work towards fostering a more compassionate and supportive community that uplifts and empowers individuals on their spiritual journey.

Allah, the Lord of Mercy

> Allah, the Exalted, has said: 'O child of Adam! I shall go on forgiving you so long as you pray to Me and aspire for My forgiveness whatever may be your sins. O son of Adam! I do not care even if your sins should pile up to the sky and should you beg pardon of Me, I would forgive you. O son of Adam! If you come to Me with an earthful of sins and meet Me, not associating anything with Me in worship, I will certainly grant you as much pardon as will fill the earth.[27]

Allah and His Prophet extend support to the wronged. They emphasise the importance of mercy and forgiveness, even to the extent of rendering the good deeds of the pious ineffective when they oppress or humiliate the sinner. A poignant example is illustrated in the words of the Prophet Muhammad (peace be upon him). Once someone swore by Allah that he would not forgive his sinful brother. At this, Allah, the Exalted and the Glorious, responded:

> Who is he that takes an oath in My Name, asserting that I will not grant pardon to so-and-so? I have indeed granted pardon to so-and-so and nullified your good deeds.[28]

The Prophet's compassionate approach is further evident in his

---
[27] *Sunan at-Tirmidhi: 1878*
[28] *Muslim, h.2621*

response to a man named Ḥimār, known to make the Prophet laugh. When brought to the Prophet due to his alcohol consumption, the Prophet defended him, saying:

> Do not insult him because he loves Allah and His Messenger.[29]

In another instance, when a man confessed to kissing and caressing a woman with mutual consent, the Prophet did not rebuke him but rather stated:

> Good deeds erase bad ones![30]

The emphasis here is not to belittle the gravity of sin but to discourage despair, as it is not in alignment with the teachings of the Quran and Sunna. Allah's preference for forgiveness over punishment is made explicit:

> When Allah created creation, He inscribed above His Throne, 'My Mercy has taken precedence over My anger.'[31]

The question arises: why would Allah punish those with broken hearts or those who are grateful and believe? The Quran provides reassurance:

> But Allah would never punish them while you, O Prophet, were in their midst. Nor would He ever punish them if they prayed for forgiveness. (Quran, 8:33)

---

[29] *Muslim: h.87*
[30] *Muslim, h.42*
[31] *Muslim, h.2751*

And:

> Why should Allah punish you if you are grateful and faithful? Allah is ever Appreciative, All-Knowing. (Quran, 4:147)

The Quran further emphasises that, despite fulfilling reasons for punishment, Allah chooses to keep us alive, providing us with a chance to rectify our wrongs:

> If Allah were to punish people immediately for their wrongdoing, He would not have left a single living being on earth. But He delays them for an appointed term. And when their time arrives, they cannot delay it for a moment, nor could they advance it. (Quran, 16:61)

Allah calls towards repentance, towards Paradise at all times:

> "And Allah invites all to the Home of Peace and guides whoever He wills to the Straight Path." (Quran, 10:25)

He does not want us to despair of His mercy:

> "We only sent messengers to be obeyed by Allah's Will. If only those hypocrites came to you O Prophet—after wronging themselves—seeking Allah's forgiveness and the Messenger prayed for their forgiveness, they would have certainly found Allah ever Accepting of Repentance,

Most Merciful." (Quran, 4:64)

The Process of Repentance

Repentance, when approached sincerely, is a profound process that goes beyond a mere tick-box exercise. For those seeking genuine repentance, it involves a heartfelt desire to mend one's ways and draw closer to the Divine. Here is a step-by-step exploration of the repentance process:

The Desire to Repent

Repentance should stem from a genuine desire to be loved by Allah, to draw close to Him, to seek salvation from Hell, and to be guided to Eden. It is not merely a duty or a way to alleviate guilt but a sincere yearning for spiritual, emotional, religious, social, physical, and financial well-being.

Objective of Repentance

The repentant individual seeks to rectify wrongs not only to adhere to a duty but to thrive in all aspects of life. Repentance is a transformative journey towards a more fulfilling existence, both in this world and the Hereafter.

Understanding Repentance

For many, repentance is a goal, while those with deeper knowledge perceive it as a means to draw closer to the Divine. The understanding of repentance goes beyond a mere obligation; it becomes a sacred pathway to spiritual growth and divine proximity.

Recognition of Sin

True repentance requires acknowledging and recognising the gravity of the sin committed. This involves an honest evaluation of one's actions and an understanding of how they have deviated from the righteous path.

Sincere Regret

Genuine repentance involves feeling a profound sense of regret for the sins committed. This regret is not merely about facing consequences but a sincere remorse for having distanced oneself from the divine guidance.

Ceasing the Sinful Behaviour

Repentance demands a practical commitment to cease the sinful behavior immediately. It is not just about remorseful words but a decisive action to discontinue the actions that led to the transgressions.

Seeking Forgiveness

Repentance involves humbly seeking forgiveness from Allah through sincere and heartfelt prayers. The repentant individual acknowledges their mistakes, seeks mercy, and implores Allah for His forgiveness.

Making Amends

Taking tangible steps to make amends for the wrongs committed is an integral part of the repentance process. This may involve restitution, seeking forgiveness from those wronged, and actively working towards positive change.

Embracing Change

Repentance is not a one-time event but a continuous process of self-improvement and spiritual growth. The repentant individual embraces positive changes in behaviour, attitude, and lifestyle to prevent a relapse into sinful patterns.

Conclusion

In essence, genuine repentance is a profound and transformative journey that involves a sincere desire for positive change, recognition of wrongdoing, heartfelt regret, immediate cessation of sinful behaviour, seeking forgiveness, making amends, and a commitment to ongoing personal growth. It is a holistic approach that addresses the spiritual, emotional, and practical dimensions of one's life.

Contents

Before you start 2
The beginning of a journey 5
Repentance and Happiness 9
The story of Wim the convert 13
Solutions to religious problems 17
An example of the prophet's (peace be upon him) psychological approach 19
   Proximity Control, Self-Examination, and Privacy 19
   Inviting perspective-taking 19
   Religious and spiritual counselling 20
Four Kinds of People in Relation to Mental Health and Spiritual Problems 22
   1. Experts in Mental Health Without a Traditional Background 22
   2. Experts in Islamic Sciences without any understanding of Mental Health 22
   3. Traditionally Educated Individuals with Basic Knowledge of Mental Health 22
   4. Mental Health Experts with Basic Knowledge of Islamic Sciences 23
   Final Remarks 23
What is Repentance? 24
Genuine repentance 29
Blossoming of True Repentance 30
   In summary: 32
Feeling guilty 33
   No mention of 'guilt' in Quran and Sunna 34
The Origin of Sin 37
Once Upon a Time When Humans Didn't Si 42

The reawakened soul	45
Summary	46
Forgiving yourself	47
The Danger of Closing the Door of Hope Upon Yourself	49
Physical Harm	49
Emotional and Physical Pain	49
Psychological Distress	49
Negative Emotional Impact	50
Distorted Beliefs	50
Social Isolation	50
Normalising Pain	50
Mental Health Risks	50
Interference with Healing	51
Misunderstanding Religious Texts and Teachings	51
The Positive Impact of Forgiving Oneself on Well-Being	52
Emotional Relief	52
Positive Thinking	52
Reward System	52
Stress Reduction	53
Brain Harmony	53
Enhanced Self-Esteem	53
Improved Relationships	53
Spiritual Growth	53
Increased Resilience	54
Inspired by al-Ghazali	55
Between self-forgiveness and acknowledging the pain inflicted on others	57
Allah does not 'feed' on the suffering of His creation	59

Personal Hurt	61
Difficulty in Coping with Personal Pain	61
Low Self-Esteem or Self-Confidence	61
Subconscious Desire for Retribution	61
Ignorance	61
Summary	62
Allah, the Lord of Mercy	63
The Process of Repentance	67
The Desire to Repent	67
Objective of Repentance	67
Understanding Repentance	67
Recognition of Sin	67
Sincere Regret	68
Ceasing the Sinful Behaviour	68
Seeking Forgiveness	68
Making Amends	68
Embracing Change	68
Conclusion	69

Printed in Great Britain
by Amazon

44304652R00047